Sinéad Huggins—Young is a Panromantic, Queer woman from Rosscarbery West Cork. She lives in Wilton with her wife Esther, her flatmates, her dog Bear, her two cats Potato and miss Vanjie and her snake Bob—Marvin.

This book is a guide to queer terminology. Contains correct terminology and slurs. It's a what to say and what not to say. The world of gay and queer terms can be difficult to navigate when it seems new terms are appearing every other day. No one is saying you must agree with them but we are saying you've got to respect a human for what they wish to be called. So, strap in and strap on for the ride of your life.

I would like to thank my lovely wife, Esther Huggins—Young for being awesome and putting up with my nonsense.

The GAY Bible

SINÉAD HUGGINS-YOUNG

AUSTIN MACAULEY PUBLISHERS™
LONDON · CAMBRIDGE · NEW YORK · SHARJAH

A CIP catalogue record for this title is available from the British Library.

ISBN 9781398466760 (Paperback)
ISBN 9781398466777 (Hardback)
ISBN 9781398466784 (ePub e-book)

www.austinmacauley.com

First Published 2022
Austin Macauley Publishers Ltd®
1 Canada Square
Canary Wharf
London
E14 5AA

I would like to thank and dedicate this book to my lovely wife Esther Huggins—Young for being awesome, putting up with my nonsense and making me a better human being. To my mum and dad Julie and John Huggins for being good parents, my in—laws Kathleen and Gordon Young who have welcomed me into their family like I'm one of their own. To my best friend Jeremiah Keyes who I can always rely on when I need to. In memory of my late brother Steven Huggins and my other best friend, my nan Elsie Lane.

The inspiration behind this book is a baby gay by the name of Rebecca Hayes, a childhood friend who I hadn't seen in years, who came out to me and did not know any of the terms from the community; a list was created and the book was born.

v

Table of content

Thank you for taking the time to read this guide to queer terminology. Is there something I am missing? You tell me, lovely human. Send an email to sineadh@ live.com and I will see if there is a need for a part two. These are just a guide to official definitions of sexuality but sexuality is fluid. One definition may be different from your own definition and that's OK too!

All sexualities are valid and should be respected. Humans should love each other. I hope you find this amusing and informative, my loves, from your friendly neighbourhood queer!

Abrosexual

An abrosexual is an individual that as a fluid or rapidly changing sexuality that fluctuates between different sexualities.

Abrosexual pride flag:

AC/DC

The actual term 'AC/DC' officially stands for Alternating Current/Direct Current. Something that was labelled AC/DC was able to receive power from either method. So, therefore, AC/DC has become a popular slang term for bisexuality, as a bisexual person is open to either sex, just like AC/DC devices are open to both currents.

Ace Cards

Asexual people use the Ace playing cards as symbols for their specific orientation as 'Ace' is a phonetic shortening of 'Asexual'. The ace of spades is for aromantic asexuals, the ace of hearts is for romantic asexuals, the ace of clubs is for graysexuals and grayromantics and the ace of diamonds is for demiromantics and demisexuals.

Agender

A person who does not identify themselves as having a particular gender.

Agender pride flag:

Ally

An ally/straight ally is a heterosexual, cisgender person who supports gender equality, and LGBTQ+ people, challenging homophobia, biphobia, and transphobia.

Straight ally pride flag:

Alphabet Mafia

The alphabet mafia is a slightly controversial term used to refer to LGBTQ+ people. The bigots who created the term alphabet mafia intended it to demonise non—heteronormative people. However, the LGBTQ+ community have taken it as their own term and it's used as a humorous way to describe yourself as a community member.

Androgynous

Androgyny is the combination of masculine and feminine characteristics into an ambiguous form. Androgyny may be expressed about biological sex, gender identity, or gender expression.

Androgynous pride flag:

Aromanticism/Aros

Aromanticism is a state of experiencing romantic love or romantic attraction to others, and such a person is called an alloromantic. An informal term for an aromantic person is aro.

Aromantic pride flag:

Artiste

This term refers to a gay male who excels at gay oral sex. It is slang used by gay men for each other. It is not believed to be a common or frequently used term in gay culture.

Asexual/Aces

Asexual orientation is generally characterised by not feeling sexual attraction or a desire for partnered sexuality. This does not mean ace people do not have sex, they may engage in sex for the sake of their partner or for other reasons.

Auntie

Auntie is a term described as an older, often effeminate and gossipy gay man. It is someone younger gay men may call upon for advice as they have lived through many queer events and have the knowledge the community will seek out.

Baby Dyke

A lesbian girl who looks or who is younger than the age of 18. Baby dykes are usually quite feminine looking and acting but will often have short hair. Some can be baby bull dykes i.e. hypermasculine younger lesbians.

Bathhouses

Bathhouses were frequented by gay men for sexual encounters in ancient Rome. There are still to this day bathhouses all around the world that accommodate such activities.

Bathsheba

A Bathsheba is a gay man who frequents gay bathhouses for sexual encounters.

Baby Gay

Someone who has just come out of the closet recently. 1–2 years is the time span of when someone could be qualified as a baby gay. Baby gays usually instantly love everything that's rainbow and just generally have that innocent glee of just coming out. We must protect them. For example, "This book is perfect for the fresh–faced baby gay."

Batty Boy

In Jamaican Patois, batty boy (Also batty boy, batty man, and chi bwoy/man) is a derogatory word often used to refer to a gay or effeminate man. The term derives from the Jamaican slang word batty, which refers to buttocks or anus.

BDSM

BDSM is a variety of often erotic practices or roleplaying involving bondage, discipline, dominance, submission, sadomasochism, and other related interpersonal dynamics.

Beanie

A beanie is a type of hat commonly worn by the lesbian community.
There is a longstanding joke that when you come out as a lesbian that you must collect your beanie and plaid shirt, which is a common dress amongst lesbians.

Beach Bitch

This term refers to a gay man who frequents beaches and resorts for sexual encounters. It is more common to hear American gay men using this term as it originates there.

Bear Chaser

A bear chaser is a gay man who pursues, seeks out or is mainly into or just into bears in the community.

Bear

A bear is a larger and hairier man who projects an image of rugged masculinity. However, in San Francisco during the 1970s, any hairy man of whatever shape was referred to as a 'bear' until the term was appropriated by larger men.

Bear pride flag:

Beat

Beat is an Australian term meaning a gay man having or seeking anonymous gay sex. This term is solely used in the Australian gay community and is not used around the world.

Beard

Beard is an American slang term describing a person who is used, knowingly or unknowingly, as a date, romantic partner or spouse either to conceal infidelity or to conceal one's sexual orientation.

Bent

Bent is a slur invented by heterosexual people meaning the opposite of straight. The word is othering and separating gay people from straight people and has been reclaimed by some members of the LGBTQ+ community but is still seen as an offensive word by most LGBTQ+ people and should not be used when referring to anyone. The term 'straight as an arrow' also comes from straight people making themselves the opposite of LGBTQ+ people.

Bi- Erasure

Bisexual erasure is the tendency to ignore, remove, falsify, or re-explain evidence of bisexuality in history or the media. In its most extreme form, bisexual erasure can include the belief that bisexuality does not exist. It may include the assertion that all bisexual individuals are in a phase and will soon choose a side. Gross misrepresentations of bisexual individuals as hypersexual, erases the sexual agency of bisexuals, effectively erasing their true identities as well.

Bicon

A bicon is an iconic bisexual individual. Someone (Usually a celebrity or an activist) that other bisexual and queer people can look up to. For example, Kirsten Stewart, Lady Gaga and Jason Mraz.

Bigender

Bigender people experience exactly two gender identities, either simultaneously or varying between the two. These two gender identities could be male and female but could also include non-binary identities.

Bigender pride flag:

Biological/Assigned Sex

In general terms, 'sex' refers to the biological differences between males and females, such as genitalia and genetic differences i.e. your assigned sex at birth.

BIFI

BIFI is the bisexual equivalent of gaydar. It means if someone has good BIFI, they can tell when another person is bisexual or not. Many bisexual people will say they can tell if someone has 'bi energy' or 'bi vibes', meaning they are saying/doing something stereotypical bisexuals will do.

Biphobia

Biphobia is an aversion towards bisexuality and bisexual people as individuals. It can be a denial that bisexuality is a genuine sexual orientation or of negative stereotypes about people who are bisexual (Such as the beliefs that they are promiscuous or dishonest). It is common for bisexual men to be believed not to exist as they are seen to be gay and just at a denial stage, this is false and is damaging to bisexual men.

Binding

Chest binding is the act of flattening breasts with constrictive materials. The term also refers to the material used in this act. Common binding materials include cloth strips and purpose–built undergarments, often using spandex. The act of breast binding is common for transmen to aid with gender dysphoria but is also done by androgynous and non–binary people.

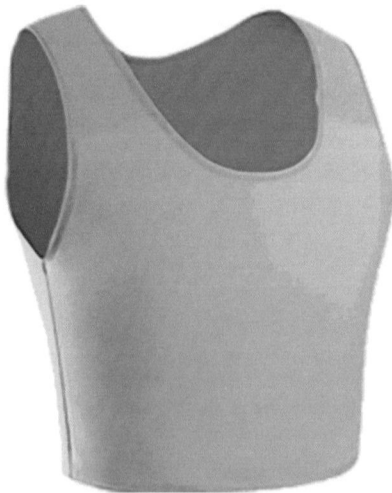

Bisexual

A person who is strictly attracted to the male and female genders. Bisexuality is romantic attraction or sexual attraction toward both males and females.

Bisexuality symbol:

Bisexual pride flag:

Black Rings

Black rings are worn by asexual people to signal to others that they are asexual. They are often seen with ace cards on them.

Black rings:

Bottom

A bottom is usually the receptive partner during sexual penetration. This frequently refers to gay men who are penetrated via the anus during anal sex. Bottoming is also used as a verb meaning 'to be penetrated by another'.

BOI

This is a term that originates in the UK. The term BOI may be used for sexual orientations and possibilities such as a boyish lesbian, a submissive butch in the BDSM community, a young transman/a transman who is in the earlier stages of transitioning, a younger bisexual or gay person who may have effeminate characteristics. The term can also be used by anyone who wishes to distinguish from heterosexual or heteronormative identities.

Bottom Surgery

The array of medically indicated surgeries differs between transwomen (MTF) and transmen (FTM). For transwomen, genital reconstruction usually involves the surgical construction of a vagina. For transmen, genital reconstruction may involve the construction of a penis. Not all transgender people will opt or need to go through this operation to complete their transitioning.

Breeder

Breeder is a satirical term coined by the gay community particularly for straight parents who purportedly overfocus on their children and allegedly abandon their previous friends and lifestyle or to women who give birth to many children, often with the derisive implication that they have too many offspring. It has been described as a joking or derogatory slur used by gays to describe heterosexuals.

Brownie Queen

A brownie queen is a gay man who prefers a passive role in anal intercourse. This is a term mainly used in American gay culture.

Bucket Boy

Bucket boy is another American gay culture term for a passive male partner in anal intercourse and is a term used specifically in America.

Butch

The term butch tends to denote a degree of masculinity displayed by a female individual beyond what would be considered typical of a tomboy. It is common for women with a butch appearance to face harassment as it is the stereotype of a lesbian in the community.

Butch pride flag:

Bussy

Slang term used by gay men to connote Boy–Pussy. In reference to their anus. Bussy has been used for at least 15 years by gay men to describe their butt.

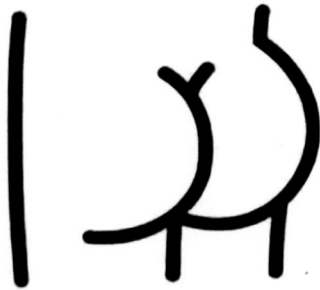

Butt Plug

A butt plug is a sex toy that is designed to be inserted into the rectum for sexual pleasure. They are like a dildo in some ways but tends to be shorter and have a flanged end to prevent the device from being lost inside the rectum.

Cafeteria

This refers to the act of repeated fellatio/gay male oral sex in a backroom or bathhouse. This is solely an American term and is not used around the world.

Camp

When the usage appeared in 1909, it denoted 'ostentatious, exaggerated, affected, theatrical, effeminate or homosexual' behaviour. It is the main description of the stereotypical gay man. However, it is not only used for homosexual people.

Cake

Cake is a symbol associated with asexuality inside of the community. It is thought to be linked to the proverbial choice between cake and sex because asexual people would probably choose cake.

Carpet Muncher/Rug Muncher

This is a very vulgar and offensive term for a person who performs oral sex on a woman, usually a lesbian. The 'carpet' or 'rug' refers to pubic hair on a woman. This is a term that should never be used when referring to anyone.

Celesbian

A celesbian is a celebrity lesbian, they can commonly be found on TIK TOK, YouTube or other social media platforms and their main content is queer−related and community−based.

Chem—sex

Chem—sex is using drugs as part of your sex life and it's most common among gay and bi men. There are typically three specific 'chems' (Drugs) involved. People say these drugs make them feel less inhibited and increase pleasure. The three main drugs people take as part of chem—sex are methamphetamine, mephedrone and GHB/GBL.

Chubby Chaser

A chubby chaser is a gay man who pursues, seeks out or is into mainly or just into overweight gay men in the community.

Cisgender

A cisgender person is a person whose gender identity matches their sex assigned at birth. For example, someone who identifies as a woman and was identified as female at birth is a cisgender woman. The word cisgender is the antonym of transgender.

Cis–Hets

An abbreviation of cisgendered heterosexual; a person that identifies as the sex they were born as and are attracted to people of the opposite sex.

Cliterference

This is the female version of cock block. When someone is standing in the way of a girl who wants to hook up with another person with a vagina. In the lesbian and bisexual community, it is used in reference to an ex–partner who gets in the way of you hooking up with a new partner. "My ex needs to stop with her cliterference."

Closeted

Closeted and in the closet are metaphors for LGBTQ+ people who have not disclosed their sexual orientation or gender identity and aspects of themselves including sexual identity and sexual behaviour. It can also be used to describe anyone who is hiding part of their identity because of social pressure or family situation.

Clone

Popularised in the 80s, a clone refers to a San Franciscan or New York Greenwich Village denizen with exaggerated macho behaviour and appearance. Freddie Mercury was known for his clone appearance.

Copenhagen Capone

This is an American term used for a transsexual person who has been castrated either at birth or later in adulthood.

Consent

Consent occurs when one person voluntarily agrees to the proposal or desires of another. It is a term of common speech, with specific definitions as used in such fields as sexual relationships. For example, a person with a mental disorder, a low mental age, or under the legal age of sexual consent may willingly engage in a sexual act that still fails to meet the legal threshold for consent as defined by applicable law.

Cottage/Cottaging

A cottage is a reference meaning public toilet where gay men engage in sex. Cottaging is the act of going to a cottage for gay sex.

Cottage Core Lesbian

Broadly speaking, it means running away from capitalism to live on a farm with your lesbian wife. As cottage core has risen in popularity, a spin—off wave of Tik Toks, created by so—called 'cottage core lesbians' have emerged.

Cottage core lesbian pride flag:

Cotton Ceiling

Cotton ceiling is a term that is used when a lesbian refuses to have sex with a transwoman, particularly if the transwoman has not undergone sex affirmation surgery.

Crossdressing

Crossdressing is the act of wearing items of clothing not commonly associated with one's sex. Crossdressing has been used for purposes of disguise, comfort, comedy, and self–expression in modern times and throughout history. Almost every human society throughout history has had expected norms for each gender relating to style, colour, or type of clothing they are expected to wear defining what type of clothing is appropriate for each gender.

Cruise

A person who is cruising is someone looking to have casual sexual encounters with the same sex. The term is more popular in the male gay scene. It is the intended purpose for applications such as Grindr.

Cub

A younger (Or younger-looking) version of a bear is called a cub. A cub can be hairy or not. He typically has (But not always) a smaller frame. The term is sometimes used to imply the passive partner in a relationship. Their flag is very similar to the bear pride flag except for the addition of the male symbol.

Cub pride flag:

Daddy

A daddy in gay culture is a slang term meaning a typically older man sexually involved in a relationship or wanting sex with a younger male. The age gap may differ, but the relationship involves the traditional parental hierarchy of father-son dynamics, the daddy providing emotional support and guidance along with sexual encouragement and nurturing to the inexperienced or sometimes vulnerable partner.

In the female world it usually refers to a butch lesbian who engages in "thirst traps" on TIKTOK.

Deadnaming

Deadnaming occurs when someone intentionally or not, refers to a person whose transgender by the name they used before they transitioned. You may also hear it described as referring to someone by their 'birth name' or their 'given name'. This is considered the ultimate disrespect in the trans community. This also can apply to non−binary people.

Demiromantic

Demiromantic is a romantic orientation on the aromantic spectrum defined as someone who does not experience romantic attraction until they have formed a deep emotional connection with someone. The connection can be sexual or platonic.

Demiromantic pride flag:

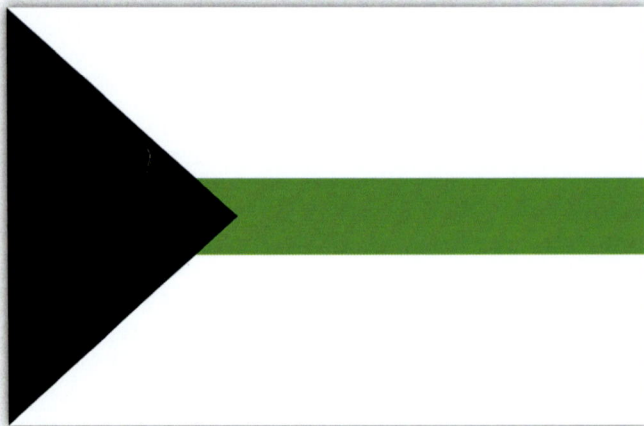

Death Drop

A move that's in dance, usually to end a dance but can be in the middle of the dance. It's a dramatic fall into a strike pose or another death drop is a kick death drop which is the same thing but ending in a different pose. One leg is behind the performer while the other is facing outwards. This was popularised by the show RuPaul's Drag Race.

Detransition

Detransition is the cessation or reversal of a transgender identification or gender transition, whether by social, legal or medical means. Some individuals detransition on a temporary basis. Desistance is a related term used to describe the cessation of transgender identity or gender dysphoria and has a higher occurrence. Research suggests that only 1.8% of people who have transitioned have detransitioned.

Demisexual

Demisexuality is a sexual orientation where people only experience sexual attraction to people that they have close emotional connections with. In other words, demisexual people only experience sexual attraction after an emotional bond has formed.

Demisexual pride flag:

Dominatrix

A dominatrix is a woman who takes the dominant role in BDSM activities. A dominatrix might be of any sexual orientation but her orientation does not necessarily limit the genders of her submissive partners. The role of a dominatrix may not even involve physical pain toward the submissive; her domination can be verbal, involving humiliating tasks or servitude.

Doe/Stag

A doe is a bisexual woman who performs femininity for themselves and themselves only. A stag is a bisexual woman who rejects femininity for themselves and themselves only.

Down Low

This term is used in black gay American culture to describe homosexual or bisexual activity, kept secret by men who have sex with men. It has however been claimed by some straight people to keep quiet about something.

Dopplebanger

This is a lesbian slang term used to describe two people dating who look exactly the same. They can also have the same exact personality or name. It is a common stereotype within the lesbian community.

Drag King

Drag kings are mostly female performance artists who dress in masculine drag and personify male gender stereotypes as part of an individual or group routine. A typical drag show may incorporate dancing, acting, stand–up comedy and singing, either live or lip–synching to pre–recorded tracks. Drag kings often perform as exaggeratedly macho male characters, portraying marginalised masculinities such as construction workers and rappers.

Drag Her

A popularised term in gay culture often refers to the humiliation of a person. It's a way of throwing shade. For example, if someone said, "Girl, look how orange you look." Someone might respond, "YASSS QUEEN! Drag her!"

Drag Queen

A drag queen is a male who uses drag clothing and makeup to imitate and often exaggerate female gender signifiers and gender roles for entertainment purposes. Drag shows frequently include lip–syncing, live singing, and dancing. They occur at events like gay pride parades and drag pageants and in venues such as cabarets and nightclubs.

Dykon

This term refers to a celebrity woman who is seen as an icon by lesbians and she may or may not be a lesbian herself. For example, Ellen DeGeneres, Sigourney Weaver and Ruby Rose.

Dyke

The term dyke is a slang term meaning lesbian. It originated as a homophobic and misogynistic slur for masculine, butch, or androgynous women. Pejorative use of the word still exists but the term dyke has been re—appropriated by many lesbians to imply assertiveness and toughness or simply as a neutral synonym for lesbian, although not every lesbian agrees with the use of the term.

Egg

An egg is a suspected transgender person who has not realised they're trans yet. It is used by transgender people when aspects of one's personality or behaviour remind them of gender—related aspects of themselves before they realised, they were trans.

Faggot

Faggot, often shortened to fag, is a usually pejorative term used primarily to refer to gay men and boys. Around the turn of the 21st century, its meaning extended as a broader reaching insult more related to masculinity and group power structure. The use of fag and faggot has spread from the United States to varying extents elsewhere in the English—speaking world through mass culture, including film, music, and the internet. It is the ultimate no—no.

Facial Feminisation Surgery

Facial feminisation surgery (FFS) is a set of cosmetic surgical procedures that alter typically male facial features to bring them closer in shape and size to typical female facial features. FFS can include various bone and soft tissue procedures such as brow lift, rhinoplasty, cheek implantation, and lip augmentation. Faces contain secondary sex characteristics that make male and female faces readily distinguishable.

Fairy

A fairy is a term that refers to a stereotypically gay man; it was a slur that has been reclaimed by gay men in the 1960s. However, some members of the community still find the term extremely offensive.

Fag–Hag

This is an offensive term used to describe a heterosexual woman who spends much of her time with gay men.

Femdom

Literally female domination. Femdom is when the female in the partnership is sexually in charge. It can include bondage, S&M and B&M. Often found with feet worship. The dominatrix can either oversee a male or a female. Femdom is popular in lesbian groups.

Femdom pride flag:

Fem

Femme/high femme is a term used to describe a lesbian who exhibits a feminine identity. It is sometimes used by/for feminine gay men, bisexuals, and transgender individuals. The word femme itself comes from the French word meaning 'woman'.

Fish

A fish is a term that 'drag queens' coined, meaning a drag queen who is effeminate enough to pass as a cisgender woman/someone who was assigned female at birth.

Flamer

A flamer is an offensive American word that should not be used for an effeminate gay man. Straight people used this term to describe a gay man who was acting extremely flamboyantly. Someone who wore very bright clothing, had loud speech, upbeat attitude, often being described as noisy, annoying, or intrusive.

Friend of Dorothy

In gay slang, a 'friend of Dorothy' (FOD) is a gay man and more broadly, any LGBTQ+ person. Stating that, or asking if, someone was a friend of Dorothy was a euphemism used for discussing sexual orientation without others knowing its meaning. The term is believed to originate from the prequel to *The wizard of oz* called *The road to oz*.

Fruit

A fruit is a slur against gay men; originally a stereotype of gay men as 'softer' and 'smelling good'. It was invented by heterosexual homophobes.

Fruit Fly

People who associate often with lesbian, gay, bisexual and transgender people may be called fruit flies (Along with fruit bats) regardless of their sex. Fruit fly can also refer to a gay man.

FTM/MTF

FTM means female to male and MTF means male to female. These are terms regarding transgender people, dependent on which way they are transitioning.

Furries

Furries are individuals who are especially interested in anthropomorphic or cartoon animals. Both sexual attraction to anthropomorphic animals and sexual arousal by fantasizing about being anthropomorphic animals. It can also be platonic and a form of escapism from the "real world".

Furries pride flag:

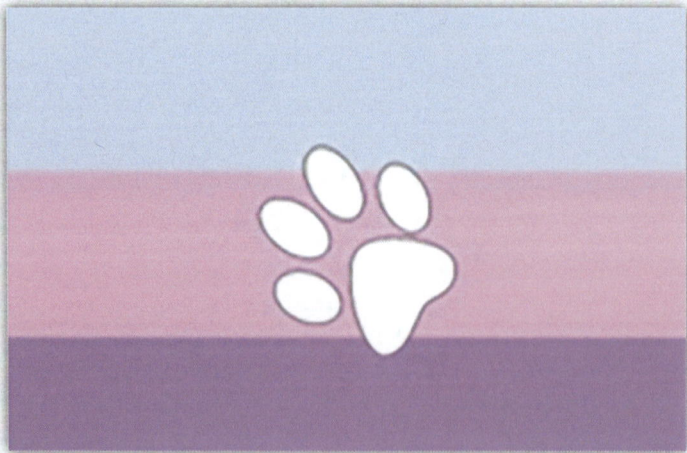

Fudge Packer

A fudge packer is an offensive slang used to describe a gay man who practices anal sex. Do not use the term for anyone.

Gaydar

Gaydar is a colloquialism referring to the intuitive ability of a person to assess others' sexual orientations as gay, bisexual or straight. Gaydar relies on verbal and non-verbal clues and LGBTQ+ stereotypes. These include the sensitivity to social behaviours and mannerisms.

Gay

Gay is a term that primarily refers to a homosexual person or the trait of being homosexual. The term originally denoted being 'carefree', 'cheerful' or 'bright and showy'. This mainly refers to gay men but the term has been used as an umbrella term for the community.

Gay male pride flag:

Gaysian

A gaysian is a gay slang term for a gay Asian person, usually referencing a gay male person.

Gaymer

Gaymer and gay gamer are umbrella terms used to refer to the group of people who are identified as gay and have an active interest in video games or tabletop games, also known as gamers. LGBTQ+ gamers are often categorised under this term.

Gender Expression

Gender expression/gender presentation is a person's behaviour, mannerisms, interests and appearance that are associated with gender in a particular cultural context, specifically with the categories of femininity or masculinity. This also includes gender roles. These categories rely on stereotypes about gender.

Gender Dysphoria

Gender dysphoria is the distress a person feels due to a mismatch between their gender identity and the sex they were assigned at birth. The diagnostic label gender identity disorder was used until 2013. The condition was renamed to remove the stigma associated with the term disorder. People with gender dysphoria commonly identify as transgender.

Gender Non—conforming/Gender Variant

Gender variance/gender non—conformity is behaviour or gender expression by an individual that does not match masculine or feminine gender norms. People who exhibit gender variance may be called gender—variant, gender—nonconforming, gender—diverse, gender—atypical or non—binary.

Gender Identity

Gender identity is the personal sense of one's own gender. Gender identity can correlate with a person's assigned sex at birth or can differ from it. Gender expression typically reflects a person's gender identity, but this is not always the case. While a person may express behaviours, attitudes, and appearances consistent with a particular gender role, such expression may not necessarily reflect their gender identity.

Genderfluid

Genderfluid people often express a desire to remain flexible about their gender identity rather than committing to a single definition. They may fluctuate between different gender expressions over their lifetime or express multiple aspects of various gender markers at the same time.

Genderfluid pride flag:

Genderqueer

Genderqueer is a gender identity that's built around the term 'queer'. To be queer is to exist in a way that may not align with heterosexual or homosexual norms. Although it's typically used to describe a person's sexual orientation, it can also be used to express a non–binary identity.

Genderqueer pride flag:

Gold Star Gay

A person who only slept with someone of the same gender i.e. a lesbian who has only ever slept with women or a gay man who has only slept with men.

Graysexual

The term is intentionally vague to accommodate the people who fall somewhere between asexual and sexual. They might experience sexual attraction occasionally, but largely does not. A graysexual person may have a history of sexual experience that doesn't reflect their current sexual identity or sense of self.

Graysexual pride flag:

Grindr

Grindr is a location—based online dating application for gay, bi, trans, and queer people. It was one of the first apps for gay men when it launched in March 2009 and has since become the largest and most popular gay mobile app in the world.

GUG

Gay until graduation is an American term to usually describe a teenager who is a man or woman who experiments with bisexual or homosexual activity during school and college only.

Henny

Henny or hunty is a word that drag queens often call each other as a casual and friendly word i.e. "Yassssss hunty" or "What's up, henny?" It gained popularity from the TV show RuPaul's Drag Race.

Heterophobia

Heterophobia is a made-up concept by straight people meaning that gay people have an aversion to or dislike towards straight people. This is not fact but some LGBTQ+ people may be wary of some straight people as they could have had negative experiences with homophobic people in the past.

Hermaphrodite

In reproductive biology, a hermaphrodite is an organism that has complete/partial reproductive organs and produces gametes normally associated with both male and female sexes. In the LGBTQ+ community, it is an outdated and somewhat offensive term for someone who is intersex and should never be used when referring to someone who is intersex.

Heterosexual

Someone who is attracted to someone of the opposite gender. Also known as straight.

Homo/Heteroflexible

Homoflexible refers to someone who is mostly homosexual but sometimes is sexually attracted to the opposite sex. Heteroflexible refers to one who is mostly heterosexual but sometimes sexually attracted to the same sex.

Homoflexible pride flag (Inverted for heteroflexible):

Horatian

A term with unknown origin, Horatian means a bisexual male. Bisexual males are often believed not to exist rather they are believed to just be gay and are not admitting it to themselves. This is false, bisexual men exist but often fear coming out even in the LGBTQ+ community for fear of not being believed but they are just as valid as everyone else.

Homophobia

It does not mean someone who is afraid of the gays! Homophobia encompasses a range of negative attitudes and feelings towards homosexuality or people who are identified or perceived as being LGBTQ+. It has been defined as contempt, prejudice, aversion, hatred or antipathy, maybe based on irrational fear and ignorance, and is often related to religious beliefs.

Hormone Replacement Therapy (HRT)

Transgender hormone therapy is a form of
hormone therapy in which sex hormones
and other hormonal medications are given to
transgender or gender nonconforming individuals
for the purpose of more closely aligning their
secondary sexual characteristics with their
gender identity. Oestrogen is given to trans
AMAB people and testosterone is given to trans
AFAB people.

In The Closet

Closeted and in the closet are metaphors for LGBTQ+ people who have not disclosed their sexual orientation or gender identity and aspects of themselves such as sexual identity and sexual behaviour. It can also be used to describe anyone who is hiding part of their identity because of social pressure. An unpopular slur for pansexual people is coming out of the cupboard because of the prefix 'pan'; this is considered offensive.

Intersex

Intersex people are born with chromosomes, gonads, sex hormones or genitals that do not fit the typical M/F genitalia at birth. Parents were once told to raise the child as a certain gender depending on what their genitals looked most like at birth, which has now been proven to damage the mental health of intersex people.

Intersex pride flag:

Kai–Kai

'Kai–Kai' refers to when two drag queens or two drag kings engage in sexual activity or 'hook up' whilst in full drag i.e. dressed as the opposite sex. The term most likely derives from the American slang term 'ki', which is a general term used when gay men laugh or joke around with one another.

Ki–Ki

'Kiki' (Alternately kiking) is a term that grew out of Black American gay social culture and is loosely defined as a gathering of friends for the purpose of gossiping and chit–chat and later made more widely known in the song *Let's Have a Kiki* by the Scissor Sisters.

Labels

Any queer acronym i.e. LGBTQ+. Not Labelling sexuality, Pomosexual: A term (Not necessarily an identity) used to refer to those who reject sexuality labels or don't identify with any of them.

Pomosexual pride flag

Ladyboy

Ladyboy is the English translation for kathoey. It is a Thai term that is very close to being the equivalent of a transgender woman. It can also encapsulate effeminate gay men. Kathoeys have been around forever in Thailand. The phenomenon is nothing new.

Le$bian/Le Dollar Bean

Le$bian or le dollar bean is a popular TIK TOK trend that involves le$bian influencers making LGBTQ+ content and when uploading, the voice over called it out as "le dollar bean" instead of le$bian. The use of le$bian is now popularised by community influencers.

Lemon

In Australia, the term lemon is referring a lesbian. This expression is not negative and is commonly used among lesbians. The origin of this slang word is unknown but is popular down under.

Leather Community

The leather subculture denotes practices and styles of dress organised around sexual activities that involve leather garments, such as leather jackets, vests, boots, chaps, harnesses, or other items. Many participants associate leather culture with BDSM.

Leather pride flag:

Lesbian

A lesbian is a homosexual woman. The word lesbian is also used for women in relation to their sexual identity or sexual behaviour, regardless of sexual orientation, as female homosexuality or same-sex attraction.

Lesbian pride flag:

Lesbian Bed Death

Lesbian bed death is the concept that lesbian couples in committed relationships have less sex than any other type of couple or stop having sex altogether. The stereotype of longer the relationship lasts lesbian couples generally experience less sexual intimacy consequently. However this has been proven as false.

Lipstick lesbian

Lipstick lesbian is slang for a lesbian who exhibits a greater amount of feminine gender attributes, such as wearing make-up, dresses or skirts, and having other characteristics associated with feminine women. In popular usage, the term is also used to characterize the feminine gender expression of bisexual women, or the broader topic of female-female sexual activity among feminine women.

Lipstick lesbian pride flag:

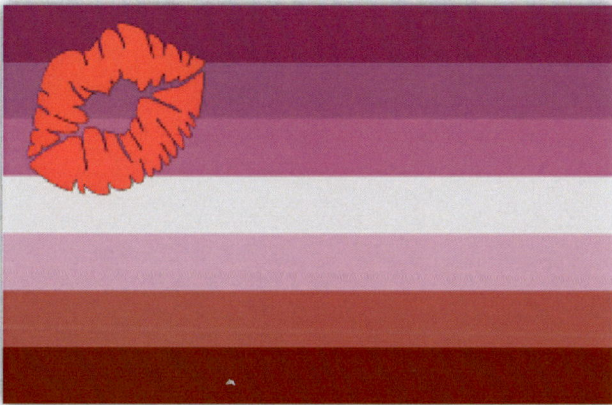

Looking

Slang in male gay dating apps, meaning 'Are you looking to hook up?' Or have sex immediately.

LUG

Lesbian until graduation is an American term to usually describe a teenager who is a woman who experiments with bisexual or homosexual activity during school only.

Manatee

The word manatee describes a big, hairless gay man, i.e. a bear without hair.

Manatee pride flag:

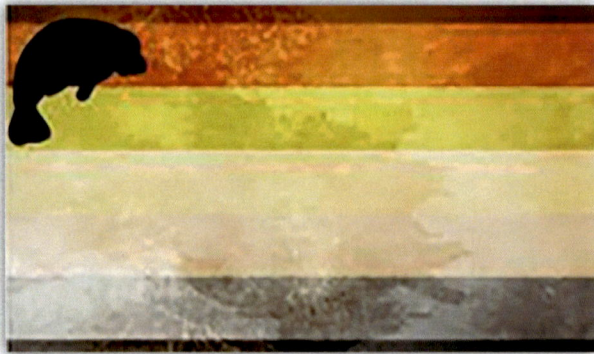

Metoidioplasty

Metoidioplasty, also known as meta, is a term used to describe surgical procedures that work with your existing genital tissue to form a penis. It can be performed on anyone with significant clitoral growth from the use of testosterone.

Merkin

A merkin is a pubic wig. Merkins were originally worn by sex workers after shaving their pubic hair and are now used as decorative items, erotic devices or in films by both men and women.

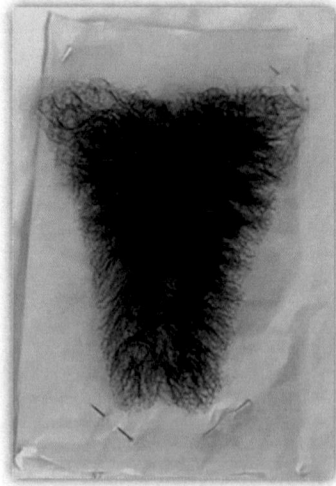

Mince/Mincing

'Mincing' describes actions that a man might make which appear to be odd or even give the impression of femininity. It can be very offensive to use this outdated language.

Miss Vanjie

Vanessa Vanjie Mateo, the first queen to be eliminated from her Drag Race season, made an impression on the fans with her larger—than—life attitude and her interactions in the workroom with the other queens. It was after the queen found herself sashaying away from the competition that a meme was born. Walking backward down the runway and exclaimed the now—iconic phrase "Miss Vanjie" three times before finally departing the competition.

Mother Monster

Lady Gaga or Stefani Germanotta is referred to as mother monster by her fans who are called little monsters. She is a bisexual woman who does a lot for the LGBTQ+ community. While performing a show in Russia, she was told by government officials not to mention anything gay-related or she would be arrested, which was the first thing she did when she got onto the stage telling her fans, "Tonight this is my house, Russia, and you can be gay in my house."

Muff Diver

A woman who is to perform cunnilingus on another woman. However, the term is also used in a derogatory way towards butch lesbian women. It is an outdated slur that should not be used when referring to lesbian women.

Nancy Boy/Pansy

A derogatory slur when referring to an effeminate man, especially an effeminate homosexual. This is an offensive term that should never be used when referring to gay men.

Neutrois

Neutrois is a gender identity characterised by gender neutrality, such neutrality or neutral gender is often translated as indifference towards gender or even lack of it (Nullity), as in agender.

Neutrois pride flag:

Non–Binary

A non–binary person identifies with a gender outside of the 'male/female gender binary', such as an agender person, who's identity is gender–neutral rather than specifically male or female.

Non–binary pride flag:

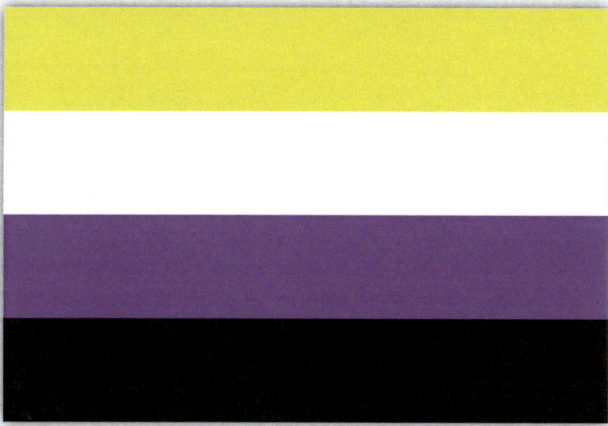

NPNC

Another male gay dating app term. It is the abbreviation of 'No pic, no chat'. Commonly used in one's profile bio meaning, if your profile does not have a picture up then you are not willing to chat.

Omnisexual

Omnisexuality is a sexual orientation where one is attracted to all genders or any gender, though gender often still plays a role or a preference in one's attraction. Similar to pansexuality.

Omnisexual pride flag:

Otter

An otter is a thinner, hairier gay man. It is a subculture of the bear community.

Otter pride flag:

Outing/Being Outed

Outing is the act of disclosing an LGBTQ+ person's sexual orientation or gender identity without that person's consent. Outing gives rise to issues of privacy, choice, hypocrisy, and harm.

Packing

Packing is the act of wearing padding or a phallic object to present the appearance of a penis. This is usually done by FTM trans people.

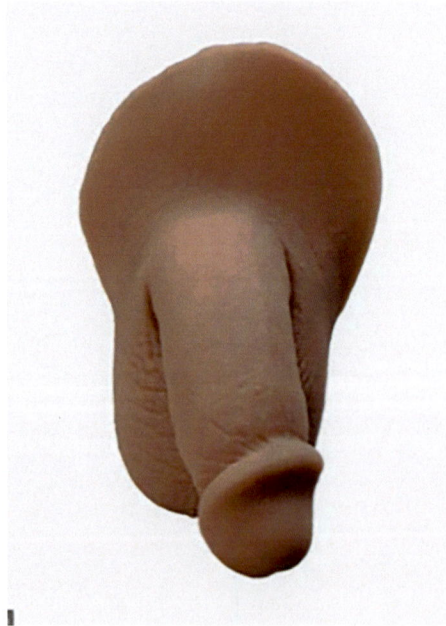

Panromantic

Someone who is panromantic is romantically attracted to people of all gender identities. This doesn't mean you're romantically attracted to everyone but that someone's gender doesn't really factor into whether you're romantically attracted to them or not.

Panromantic pride flag:

Passing

In the context of gender, passing or blending is when someone, typically a transgender person, is perceived as cisgender instead of the sex they were assigned at birth. For example, the person may be a transgender man who is perceived as a cisgender man.

Pansexual

A pansexual person is not limited in sexual choice regarding biological sex, gender or gender identity.

Pansexual symbol:

Pansexual pride flag:

PGP

A preferred gender pronoun, or PGP, is simply the pronoun or set of pronouns that an individual would like others to use when talking to or about that individual.

Phalloplasty

A phalloplasty is the construction or reconstruction of a penis. The phalloplasty is a common surgical choice for transgender and non-binary people interested in gender confirmation surgery. It's also used to reconstruct the penis in cases of trauma, cancer or congenital defect.

Pillow Princess

A pillow princess is a slang phrase that describes someone, usually an LGBTQ+ woman, who prefers to receive sexual stimulation more than they do to give it.

Plaid Shirt

A plaid shirt is commonly worn by the lesbian community. There is a longstanding joke that when you come out as a lesbian that you must collect your beanie and plaid shirt, which is a common dress amongst the lesbian community. Almost every lesbian will have one in their wardrobe.

Platinum Star Gay

A gay man who has never touched a vagina due to being born as a C–section baby.

Polish Exclusion Zone

LGBT−free zones are municipalities and regions of Poland that have declared themselves unwelcoming of an alleged 'LGBTQ+ ideology', in order to ban equality marches and other LGBTQ+ events. As of June 2020, some 100 municipalities encompassing about a third of the country, have adopted resolutions which have led to them being called "LGBT−free zones". Polish LGBTQ+ activists continue to fight the good fight against this. In fact due to the EU cutting the funding to any country that had these zones. Poland has reversed its decision to get their funding back from the EU. Homophobes 0, Gays 1.

Polyamory

Polyamory has come to be an umbrella term for various forms of non–monogamous, multi–partner relationships or non–exclusive sexual or romantic relationships. Its usage reflects the choices of the individuals involved with themes or values like love, intimacy, honesty, equality, communication, and commitment.

Polyamory pride flag:

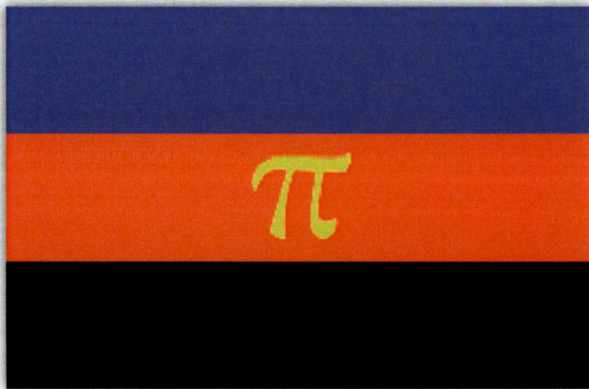

Poof/Poofter

This is another slur, an offensive term for an effeminate gay man. This term is of British origin and has been used for decades. This term should never be used to refer to or call anyone by it.

Polysexual

Polysexual individuals are attracted to people of multiple genders. People who identify as polysexual often use that word because it suggests a greater variety of sexual orientations than traditional gender binaries of male and female or hetero/homosexual.

Polysexual pride flag:

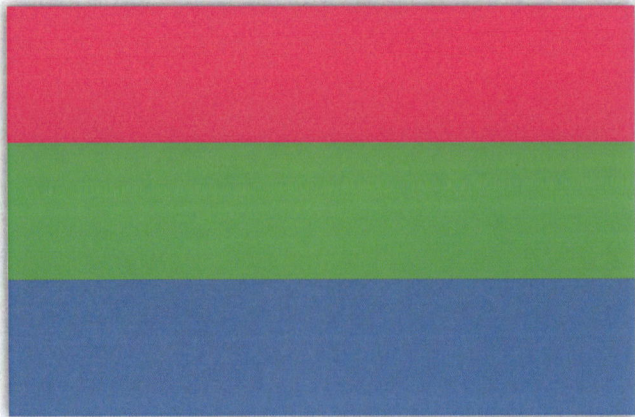

Poz

This is an American term to describe someone who is HIV positive, usually a gay male. Not widely used globally.

Power Bottom

A person who is a power bottom usually refers to a gay man who can stand being penetrated by a man/men for extended periods of time without having to take breaks as they power through it.

Pronouns

Gendered pronouns specifically reference someone's gender: he/him/his or she/her/hers. Non–binary usually goes by they/them but not always. You should always ask an LGBTQ+ person, "What are your preferred pronouns?" and if you make a mistake, it's best to acknowledge it and move on with the best effort to self–correct as you go.

Other gender pronouns used:

(f)ae	(f)aer	(f)aer	(f)aers	(f)aerself
e/ey	em	eir	eirs	eirself
he	him	his	his	himself
per	per	pers	pers	perself
she	her	her	hers	herself
they	them	their	theirs	themself
ve	ver	vis	vis	verself
xe	xem	xyr	xyrs	xemself
ze/zie	hir	hir	hirs	hirself

Pride

Pride parades are outdoor events celebrating LGBTQ+ social and self-acceptance, achievements, legal rights, and pride. Most pride events occur annually around June to honour the Stonewall riots in NYC.

First pride flag:

Modern pride flag:

Punk

A punk is a term used to describe a smaller, younger gay man who in prison settings, is forced into a submissive role and used for the older inmate's sexual pleasure.

Queen

A queen is a term used to describe an effeminate gay man; commonly used in compounds such as 'drag queen' or 'rice queen'.

Queer Baiting

Queer baiting is a marketing technique for fiction and entertainment in which creators hint at but then do not actually depict same−sex romance or other LGBTQ+ representation. They do so to attract 'bait'; a queer or straight ally audience with the suggestion of relationships or characters that appeal to them while at the same time attempting to avoid alienating other consumers.

Queer

Originally a slur against homosexuals, transgender people and anyone who does not fit society's standards of gender and sexuality; recently reclaimed by the LGBTQ+ community and used as an umbrella term for sexual and gender minorities. You may hear the older generations of heterosexual people using this as a term for someone who is weird, strange or unusual. (The best kind of people.)

Questioning

The questioning of one's sexual orientation, sexual identity, gender, or all three is a process of exploration by people who may be unsure, still exploring, or concerned about applying a social label to themselves for various reasons. Bicurious people are people that would hook up with the same gender to see if they like it or not.

Rabbit

A rabbit vibrator (Also known as a Jack Rabbit vibrator or Jessica Rabbit vibrator) is a vibrating sex toy, usually made in the shape of a phallic shaft for vaginal stimulation with a clitoral stimulator attached to the shaft.

Reveal

On the show RuPaul's Drag Race, when the queens lip-sync, they often do either a wig reveal or an outfit reveal, where they had a second outfit or wig underneath.

Romantic Orientation

Romantic orientation indicates the sex or gender with which a person is most likely to have a romantic relationship or fall in love. It is used both alternatively and side by side with the term sexual orientation and is based on the perspective that sexual attraction is but one bit of a bigger dynamic. Although a pansexual person may feel sexually attracted to people regardless of gender. The person may experience romantic attraction and intimacy with women only.

RuPaul Drag Race

RuPaul is in search for 'America's next drag superstar'. RuPaul plays the role of host, mentor and head judge for this series, as contestants are given different challenges each week. Judges include Michelle Visage, Carson Kressley or Ross Matthews, and a host of other guest judges, who critique contestants' progress throughout the competition. The winner of each season receives $100,000 and a year's supply of make-up. The show has had a massive influence on queer culture.

Sapphic

Sapphic is used as an umbrella term for women or feminine—aligning people who are attracted to other women or feminine—aligning people. As this is an umbrella term, multiple kinds of women can use this term, like lesbians, bi women, pan women, questioning women, ace women and a whole lot of other labels could fall under this description. This is a feminine—specific identity. The term sapphic originates from Sappho, the famous lesbian poet from the island of Lesbos.

Sashay

Sashay mean to walk confidently while moving your hips from side to side in a way that attracts attention. In RuPaul's Drag race, the queens would sashay down the runway and if they were eliminated from the competition, they would be told to "sashay away".

Self–Identifying

It is what you identify as/call yourself. You assign a particular characteristic or categorisation to oneself; describe oneself as belonging to a particular category or group.

Sexual Orientation

Sexual orientation is a term used to describe a person's identity in relation to the gender or genders to which they are sexually attracted; the fact of being heterosexual, homosexual, etc.

Shade/Throwing Shade

The expressions 'throw shade', 'throwing shade', or simply 'shade' are slang terms for a certain type of insult, often non-verbal. If a person is being shady, they are often talking about you behind your back but being nice to your face.

Skliosexual

Skoliosexuality, sometimes spelled scoliosexuality, is the attraction to people who are transgender or nonbinary. People who are transgender identify as a gender different from the one they were assigned at birth. They may identify as a man, a woman, or neither.

Skliosexual pride flag:

Social Gender

Gender refers to the characteristics of women, men, girls and boys that are socially constructed. This includes norms, behaviours and roles associated with being a woman, man, girl or boy as well as relationships with each other. As a social construct, gender varies from society to society and can change over time. It can mean the gender that society sees as being socially acceptable.

Soft Butch/Stem/Stemme

These terms have the same official definition, which is an American term meaning an androgynous lesbian, in between femme and butch. However, opinions of the definition can vary, and like with every term, some people may find it offensive.

Stealth

The term stealth in its most extreme sense refers to a person who always passes as their desired sex or gender and who has broken contact with everybody who knew their gender history. It can also just mean someone who is not out as trans or someone who has transitioned and does not feel the need to tell anyone that they are a trans person.

Stonewall

The Stonewall riots (Also referred to as the Stonewall uprising or the Stonewall rebellion) were a series of spontaneous demonstrations by members of the gay (LGBTQ+) community in response to a police raid that began in the early morning hours of June 28, 1969, at the Stonewall Inn in the Greenwich Village neighbourhood of Manhattan, NYC. Patrons of the Stonewall, other LGBTQ+ bars, and neighbourhood street people fought back when the police became violent.

Stone Butch

A stone butch refers to a very masculine/butch lesbian who does not receive touch during intercourse, only giving. There is also a book called *Stone butch blues* by Leslie Feinberg which follows the narrative of the life of Jess Goldberg, who grows up in a working—class area of upstate New York in the 1940s. Her parents, frustrated with Jess's gender nonconformity, eventually institutionalise Jess in a psychiatric ward. This story has had a major influence on queer culture.

Straight Pride

Straight pride is a parade held by heterosexual people, mostly men. It is largely protested by the LGBTQ+ community as they feel there isn't a need for a straight pride and it's very insulting to the community. The straight pride organisers have been tied with neo-Nazi groups, right-wing groups and Trump supporters.

Straight pride flag:

STP

STP stands for stand to pee; a device that enables you to go to the toilet while standing up and is mainly used by trans AFAB people.

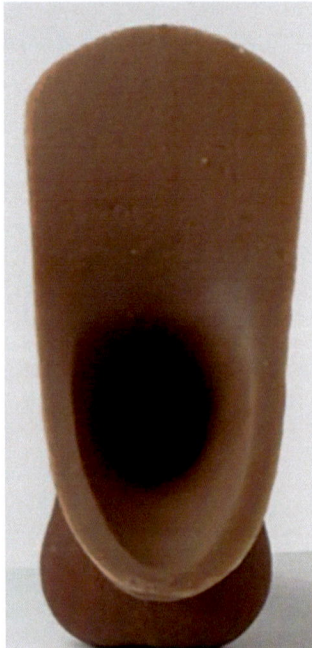

Stud

A 'stud' is a dominant lesbian. The term originated with the black lesbian community. They tend to be influenced by urban and hip-hop cultures. In the NYC lesbian community, a butch lesbian woman may identify herself as AG (Aggressive) or as a stud.

Strap-On

A strap-on is a dildo designed to be worn, usually with a harness, during sexual activity. Strap-on dildos can be used by people of any gender or sexuality.

Super Straight

This 'sexuality' started out as a TIK TOK joke but now some people are taking it seriously. The meaning of super straight is a straight person who is only attracted to cisgendered men and women of the opposite sex. It is basically for teenagers who want to be transphobic as there is usually no way to tell if someone is cisgendered or not. Someone created this jokingly as super straight (SS) the Nazi reference and the 'flag' colours are the colours of the gay dating app Grindr.

Submissive

A sub or submissive is a term related to BDSM, a submissive can be a slave and/or the bottom (The person being tied up or whipped, etc.). The dominate would control the submissive.

Swish

Swish is an American/English slang term for effeminate behaviour and interests, emphasized and sanctioned in gay male communities prior to the Stonewall riots. This behaviour is also described as being nelly in British/English and both terms are often considered to be derogatory and should not be used when referring to anyone.

Tea/Spilling Tea

Tea refers to gossip or other private information. The term is especially found in the expression spilling the tea meaning dishing out the gossip, originated from black American gay slang but is now used by most of the LGBTQ+ community.

TERF

TERF is an acronym for trans–exclusionary radical feminists. First recorded in 2008, the term applies to the minority of feminists that reject the assertion that transwomen are women, they approve of the exclusion of transwomen from women's spaces and are opposed to transgender rights legislation. The term is often used as a slur when people are showing transphobic behaviour. A TERF is seen as a very negative term by everyone except TERFS themselves.

The Straights/Straights

The Straights is a term LGBTQ+ people use to describe/insult heterosexuals and heterosexual behaviour. For example: If a straight woman were going through her boyfriend's phone because she couldn't trust him. Queer people might say, "Oh look, the straights are at it again."

Third Gender

Third gender, or third sex, is a concept in which individuals are categorised, either by themselves or by society, as neither man nor woman. It is also a social category present in societies that recognise three or more genders.

Thespian

Thespian is a fancy word for an actor. This word is related to Thespis, the guy who first took the stage in Ancient Greece. As an adjective, you can use the word thespian to describe something that is related to drama. However, the LGBTQ+ community have taken the word to mean theatre lesbian, a lesbian who participates in theatre productions.

Top

A top is a dominant or inserting sexual partner, usually in homosexual relations or activity. A top can be male, female or non–binary etc and is usually the one giving the sexual performance rather than receiving it.

Tomcat

A tomcat is a term of unknown origin meaning a woman who performs androgyny for herself and other women.

Top Surgery

Top surgery is performed on the chest as part of gender affirmation surgery, especially to remove breast tissue and produce a masculine appearance of the chest in female−to−male surgery.

Tranny

Tranny (Or trannie) is a derogatory term for a transgender, transsexual or crossdressing person and is an offensive slur in mainstream contexts. It is considered as hate speech and should never be used when talking to or about another human being.

Trans–Trender

Trans–trender is a derogatory term used to describe someone who is pretending to be transgender for attention, views on YouTube or other social media platforms or for pity which is a small portion of the non–dysphoric community. Often times, this term is used to describe someone who is transgender and does not experience gender dysphoria.

Trans AFAB/Trans AMAB

These terms are acronyms meaning 'Assigned female/male at birth'. No one, whether cis or trans, gets to choose what sex they're assigned at birth. This term is preferred to 'Biological male/ female', 'Male/female – bodied', 'Natal male/ female', and 'Born male/female', which are defamatory and inaccurate.

Transition

Gender transitioning is the process of changing one's gender presentation and/or sex characteristics to accord with one's internal sense of gender identity, the idea of what it means to be a man or a woman, or to be non–binary or genderqueer.

Transgender

Transgender is denoting or relating to a person whose sense of personal identity and gender does not correspond with their birth sex, i.e. the person they are on the inside does not match the body they were assigned at birth.

Transgender pride flag:

Transsexual

Transsexual people experience a gender identity that is inconsistent with their assigned sex and desire to permanently transition to the gender they are usually seeking medical assistance such as HRT and affirmation surgery to help them align their body with their identified sex or gender. Transsexual is a subset of transgender but some transsexual people reject the label of transgender and some transgender people reject the label transexual as they wish to separate sex and gender.

Transphobia

Transphobia is a collection of ideas and phenomena that encompass a range of negative attitudes, feelings or actions towards transgender people. Transphobia can include fear, aversion, hatred, violence, anger, or discomfort felt or expressed towards people who do not conform to social gender expectations. It does not mean people who are afraid of transgender people.

Trigender

A trigender person defines their gender identity in a third category, which is not situated in between man/woman or trigender can also mean a person who feels that they are a blending of three gender identities.

Trigender pride flag:

Tucking

Tucking is defined by the Transgender Health Information Program as ways one can hide the penis and testes, such as moving the penis and scrotum between the buttocks or moving the testes up into the inguinal canals. This is usually done by transwomen and drag queens sometimes using duct tape to hold everything in place.

Two-Spirit

Two-Spirit (Also Two spirit/two-spirited) is a modern, pan-Indian, umbrella term used by some indigenous North Americans to describe native people in their communities who fulfil a traditional third-gender (Or other gender-variant) ceremonial and social role in their cultures.

Two-spirit pride flags:

Twink

Twink is gay slang for a younger man in his late teens to early twenties whose traits may include general physical attractiveness, little to no body or facial hair, a slim to average build, and a youthful appearance.

U–Haul

The U–Haul lesbian is a stereotype of lesbian relationships, referring to the joke that lesbians tend to move in together on the second date. It suggests an extreme inclination toward monogamy or committed relationships. It can be considered either complementary or pejorative, depending on context.

Unicorn

A unicorn refers to a bisexual person (Usually a woman) who prefers to hook up with opposite–sex couples; it represents any unattainable or very few/rare things.
It's so rare to happen it is considered to be like a unicorn because basically, it doesn't exist.

Vaginoplasty

A vaginoplasty is a surgical procedure where a vagina is created. It involves removing the penis, as well as the testicles and scrotum. A vaginoplasty involves rearranging the current tissue in the genital area to create the vaginal canal and external genitalia such as the labia. To create the vaginal canal, the surgeon uses the skin from the existing penis. Sometimes, an additional skin graft from the abdomen or thigh is needed to achieve a full vaginal canal. This is a surgery for trans AMAB people.

Verse/Vers/Switch

A verse/vers/switch is a person who enjoys both topping and bottoming or being dominant and submissive and may alternate between the two in sexual situations, adapting to their partner.

Vouge

To vouge is to dance to music in such a way as to imitate the characteristic poses struck by a model on a catwalk. Commonly seen in RuPaul's Drag Race.

Werk

In Queer culture, werk means to have drive and motivation or to put in a lot of effort to something. It also means an affirmation of something. For example, "Yasssssss queen, werk!"

Wig

Wig is one of those terms that just mean anything you want it to in whatever context you're in. Wig can mean 'OK' or 'Yes, I agree'.

WLW/MLM

WLW and MLM are acronyms for women who love women and men who love men. Examples also include WLNB (woman loving non–binary). For example, lesbians, bisexual women, and pansexual women all fall under the category of women loving women WLW because they are all attracted to women and these attractions don't have to be exclusive.

Wolf

A wolf is a term used for a gay man who tends to fall evenly between a twink or a bear/cub, i.e. a gay man who is hairy and has a medium build.

Wolf pride flag:

Yas

Yas is a playful or non–serious slang term equivalent to the excited or celebratory use of the interjection "Yes!" The more As in a yas, the bigger the excitement; in other words, the exclamation often appears in the form "Yas, queen!" and as "Yaas!" or "Yaaaas!"

100–Footer

A 100–footer is a term that is used to describe someone who appears so stereotypically queer that anyone would be able to spot them from at least 100 feet away.

22/05/2015: Making History

Ireland made gay history on this day, it was the first country in the world to vote and pass a referendum that would allow same-sex marriage. Same-sex marriage in Ireland has been legal since 16 November 2015 and the first marriage ceremonies of same-sex couples in Ireland occurred the following day. Every county voted yes, except Roscommon and even then, it was a 48%–52% vote. A massive 1.2 million voters participated with people even coming home to vote from all over the world. Ireland, you did us all proud. On behalf of myself and the community, thank you!